The Deep Dark Day When Jesus Died

Words by Norman C. Habel

Pictures by Jim Roberts

P A PURPLE PUZZLE TREE BOOK

COPYRIGHT © 1973 CONCORDIA PUBLISHING HOUSE,
ST. LOUIS, MISSOURI
CONCORDIA PUBLISHING HOUSE LTD.,
LONDON, E. C. 1
MANUFACTURED IN THE UNITED STATES OF AMERICA
ALL RIGHTS RESERVED
ISBN 0-570-06548-8

Concordia Publishing House

Have you ever seen the sky turn wild
or the air reflect an orange glow? Well?
Have you ever seen a fierce black cloud
laugh and dance, like the devil in hell?

Well, the deep, dark day when Jesus died
was even more strange than that.
For that's the day the devil and sin
fought against the Son of God.

That strange, dark day began
in the house of Pilate the governor,
a miserable mouse of a man.
In front of Pilate Jesus stood,
His arms bound tight with rope,
waiting for the final word.

"Are you the king of the Jews?"
 asked Pilate the governor.
"You said it!" Jesus replied,
 and hung His head in silence.
"The man's a traitor," one priest yelled,
"and He wants to take your throne.
 He said He'd tear the temple down
 and try to build His own."

But Jesus said nothing,
nothing at all.

Then Pilate the mouse
tried to be mighty
and set poor Jesus free.
It seems that at a festival
the governor frees a prisoner
to show how great he is.
So Pilate stood before the crowd
about to give a speech.

"Give us a prisoner," the people shouted.
"Give us a gift from your throne."
"Well, what about Jesus?" Pilate replied.
"How about Jesus, your clown?"

For a moment the crowd was quiet,
until one priest screamed, "No!"
"No! No!" yelled more and more.
"We want Barabbas!
Barabbas the robber, for sure!"

"What will I do with Jesus," said Pilate,
"this clown you call your King?"
Then all the people screamed and yelled,
"Crucify Him! Crucify Him!
Crucify the King!"

Jesus stood erect and calm,
like a man with a secret inside,
who knows just who He is
and why He has to die.

Beside Him Pilate stood
as scared as a mouse inside.
He washed his hands in water
and yelled to all the crowd:
"This Jesus, friends, is innocent.
I wash His blood from my hands.
You can do what you like with Him.
He's just another man."

It was sad and dark and ugly
when they took King Jesus away.
For they didn't take Him out to die
but for ugly games they played.

They set Him on a table
before crude Roman soldiers,
rows and rows of Roman soldiers.
They stripped off all His clothes
and robed Him in a purple gown
as if He were a king.
They put a crown upon His head—
no, not a crown of gold,
but a crown of sharp, green thorns.

They laughed at Him and spat on Him
and danced in ugly glee.
They whipped Him worse than any dog
or a slave who isn't free!

But Jesus said nothing,
nothing at all.

At last they took King Jesus away
through streets of screaming people,
down the long, long road to Calvary.
They made Him carry His own cross,
but Jesus was weak with pain.

Then Jesus stumbled and fell.
The cross was much too heavy
and He was much too weak
to carry that cross on His back,
cut by the soldier's whip.

Suddenly one of the soldiers shouted,
"You! You! Come here!
Carry this cross for the Man.
You're no better than He."

That man was a man called Simon,
a traveler from Africa,
strong and black and kind.

He carried the cross of Jesus,
step by step and jeer by jeer
up the long, long hill to Calvary.
He felt the touch of Jesus' love
as He walked that road to die.

Slowly they raised the cross aloft
and Jesus felt a pain
so strong no man could take it.

While Jesus hung upon the cross,
the people kept on jeering.
"Come down from the cross, Miracle Man,
and then we'll believe," they yelled.

But Jesus said nothing,
nothing at all.

Soldiers threw their dice on the ground
while Jesus hung there dying.
They threw the dice for His clothes,
which was all He had left to give...
or was it?
For up on the cross a whisper came forth
that rang like a song through the air,
"Forgive them, Father," Jesus said.
"They don't know what they do."
Were those words a gift for us,
a promise for me and you?

When Jesus finally died,
it seemed as if the world died too.
The ground groaned and rumbled below
and tombs broke open wide.
The sky was dark as death above
and the highest heavens cried.
Dogs and donkeys whined,
while birds wailed through the night.
For everything seemed to know that day
the world had lost its life.

Will that life return again?
Will God remake the world
and bring it back to life?
I'm sure He will! Aren't you?

Will Jesus Christ return to life again
to finish the puzzle for God?

Yes, of course He will!

OTHER TITLES

SET I

WHEN GOD WAS ALL ALONE 56-1200
WHEN THE FIRST MAN CAME 56-1201
IN THE ENCHANTED GARDEN 56-1202
WHEN THE PURPLE WATERS CAME AGAIN 56-1203
IN THE LAND OF THE GREAT WHITE CASTLE 56-1204
WHEN LAUGHING BOY WAS BORN 56-1205
SET I LP RECORD 79-2200
SET I GIFT BOX (6 BOOKS, 1 RECORD) 56-1206

SET II

HOW TRICKY JACOB WAS TRICKED 56-1207
WHEN JACOB BURIED HIS TREASURE 56-1208
WHEN GOD TOLD US HIS NAME 56-1209
IS THAT GOD AT THE DOOR? 56-1210
IN THE MIDDLE OF A WILD CHASE 56-1211
THIS OLD MAN CALLED MOSES 56-1212
SET II LP RECORD 79-2201
SET II GIFT BOX (6 BOOKS, 1 RECORD) 56-1213

SET III

THE TROUBLE WITH TICKLE THE TIGER 56-1218
AT THE BATTLE OF JERICHO! HO! HO! 56-1219
GOD IS NOT A JACK-IN-A-BOX 56-1220
A LITTLE BOY WHO HAD A LITTLE FLING 56-1221
THE KING WHO WAS A CLOWN 56-1222
SING A SONG OF SOLOMON 56-1223
SET III LP RECORD 79-2202
SET III GIFT BOX (6 BOOKS, 1 RECORD) 56-1224

SET IV

ELIJAH AND THE BULL-GOD BAAL 56-1225
LONELY ELIJAH AND THE LITTLE PEOPLE 56-1226
WHEN ISAIAH SAW THE SIZZLING SERAPHIM 56-1227
A VOYAGE TO THE BOTTOM OF THE SEA 56-1228
WHEN JEREMIAH LEARNED A SECRET 56-1229
THE CLUMSY ANGEL AND THE NEW KING 56-1230
SET IV LP RECORD 79-2203
SET IV GIFT BOX (6 BOOKS, 1 RECORD) 56-123]

SET V

THE FIRST TRUE SUPER STAR 56-1242
A WILD YOUNG MAN CALLED JOHN 56-1243
THE DIRTY DEVIL AND THE CARPENTERS BOY 56-1244
WHEN JESUS DID HIS MIRACLES OF LOVE 56-1245
WHEN JESUS TOLD HIS PARABLES 56-1246
OLD ROCK THE FISHERMAN 56-1247
SET V LP RECORD 79-2204
SET V GIFT BOX 56-1248

SET VI

WONDER BREAD FROM A BOY'S LUNCH 56-1249
WHEN JESUS RODE IN THE PURPLE PUZZLE
   PARADE 56-1250
   WHEN JESUS' FRIENDS BETRAYED HIM 56-1251
   THE DEEP DARK DAY WHEN JESUS DIED 56-1252
   DANCE, LITTLE ALLELU, WITH ME 56-1253
   THE KEY TO THE PURPLE PUZZLE TREE 56-1254
   SET VI LP RECORD 79-2205
   SET VI GIFT BOX 56-1255

the PURPLE PUZZLE TREE